BEING WHOLE IN MIND AND BODY

spirit

soul

mind

body

DISCLAIMER

This eBook has been written for information purposes only. Every effort has been made to make this eBook as complete and accurate as possible. However, there may be mistakes in typography or content. Also, this eBook provides information only up to the publishing date. Therefore, this eBook should be used as a *guide* not as the ultimate source.

The purpose of this eBook is to educate. The author and the publisher do not warrant that the information contained in this eBook is fully complete and shall not be responsible for any errors or omissions. The author and publisher shall have neither liability nor responsibility to any person or entity with respect to any loss or damage caused or alleged to be caused directly or indirectly by this eBook.

This eBook offers information and is designed for educational purposes only. You should not rely on this information as a substitute, nor does it replace professional medical advice, diagnosis, or treatment.

INTRODUCTION

If you have been feeling run down with your health physically, mentally, or spiritually, you might be wondering what you can do to get back on your feet and feel whole again. Life's troubles can lead us down different paths than what we had imagined for our lives, but that does not mean we aren't capable of making changes to make our lives better.

The main goal of being whole means you need complete control of your health and life, but how is done? It can be simpler than you think when you break it down into steps and actions you can concentrate on every day.

This eBook has been put together to concentrate on the life actions and steps you can take to being whole and becoming your true self. With this eBook, you can begin to take practical actions to achieve the life and self you have always wanted.

While this book might not have all the answers for your unique situation, you can use it as a guide to bring you through a life-altering journey. It will also help you overcome your personal demons and teach you how to rely on faith to help you through life's most difficult challenges.

One Small Step
Can Change
Your Life

Chapter 1. One Small Step Can Change Your Life

Being whole and mastering your health in all forms seems like a big journey, but every journey begins with a small step. Some people choose to wait until they have everything in order to begin big life changes, but if you keep waiting, eventually you will not be able to start the journey at all. You need to start being whole with just one small change, no matter how small the step is. Remember that small steps are better than no steps, as long as you are heading in the right direction.

Stop Making Excuses

On your journey to being whole, you need to stop making excuses in order to start your first small step. One thing that drastically affects mental health in today's society and culture is the use of social media. Social media does have some important uses though, such as keeping you connected to friends and family that might be living in different parts of the world.

However, if you constantly find yourself on social media comparing yourself to others, you might need to take a break for your mental health. It's easy to make excuses when it comes to social media, but if you can't get off the screens and become more productive, you are hindering yourself from being able to take that first small step to become whole.

Quitting excuses is one of the hardest things you might ever have to do because it involves changing parts of yourself that might be set in their ways. As adults, we get stuck in habits, and many of them are distracting us from being whole.

To stop making excuses, you need to force yourself. For example, if you want to begin exercising more as part of a physical fitness journey, you need to carve out time in your schedule to make it to the gym or the park. It can be easy to make excuses, but as soon you can force yourself out of the excuses, you will be one step closer to being whole.

Setting Reasonable Goals

Making the first step means having reasonable goals and plans. If you do not set clear expectations for yourself and your goals, you will have a very hard time accomplishing them. If you want to get a new job because your current one is not boding well for your mental and spiritual health, you need to start making reasonable goals to find a new job.

One of the best ways to do this is to set a goal to send out 3 or 4 applications a week. This is reasonable for most people's timelines, but you can always adjust it to fit your schedule. While it might be tempting to tell yourself, you are going to send out 10 or 20 new applications a week, this is not usually

Practical for most people and you will only be setting yourself up for failure.

Not achieving your goals can be a huge setback when it comes to making small steps. That's why it's extremely important to make the goals clear and reasonable so that you give yourself room to accomplish them.

With reasonable goals, you can also make new habits and new lifestyles. Having goals allows you to be more productive because you are always working towards something, whether it is big or small.

Making Routines

Taking one small step also comes with creating structure and good habits for your life. You can't make good life habits without a routine. Having a routine will also help you to take small steps towards being whole because you can engage in the same discipline every day.

If you have never had a routine or schedule before, make sure to start small. For example, if you want to spend time working on your spiritual health, you can make it a habit of spending the same time every day in spiritual practices.

Maybe you wake up every morning an hour earlier so you can read a spiritual book, the Bible, or a faith-based book that you want to read. Waking up earlier every day is a simple and practical approach you can take. It's also a small step that doesn't involve too much effort.

Accountability for your Step

Once you have a routine, a step, and reasonable goals, you need to make sure you are keeping yourself accountable. If you have a hard time with this, you might also want to engage someone else to help you stay on track. Many people share their steps with a coach or friends.

You need to make sure you are creating time for accountability. This could mean sitting down at the end of every week and going over your progress. Did you wake up early every day like you said you would? Did you send in the job applications that you said you would? If not, don't be hard on yourself. But make sure you are ready for better the next week.

The Power of Small Steps

Taking a small step might seem like a big deal. You might be thinking you need to try harder or take a huge step to change your life, but most people will tell you this isn't true. Taking steps that are too big can also set you up for failure if you don't prepare correctly. It's hard to fail with small steps.

Once you complete one small step, you can take another one and another one until you have reached your goal. Taking small steps can also save you from actions that might be too risky whether it is financially or mentally.

Chapter 2. Understanding the Mind-Body Connection

If you want to be whole and reconnect with yourself spiritually, mentally, and physically, you need to understand the mind-body connection and how it affects your development. Under the mind-body connection, people believe that physical illnesses or problems come from how your mind is processing social and biological factors.

This simply means that your emotions and feelings can affect your physical health. If you have ever been in a stressful situation such as a divorce or unemployment, you probably know how stress can make your body feel worn down and slow. Stress can also affect things like blood pressure and blood sugar.

Your body can also respond to stress by having gastrointestinal issues or even stomach ulcers and headaches. You might also experience fatigue, insomnia, or shortness of breath. Many people visit the doctor thinking they have physical ailments that need to be treated, but their conditions, are actually, being caused by issues such as stress and anxiety.

Knowing how to control things like stress and anxiety can help you better manage physical symptoms and can get you into better health overall.

Improving Mind-Body Connection

Knowing that mental health can affect your physical health, you might be wondering if there are some ways you can improve the mind-body connection. There are many ways you can improve the connection, but you need to make sure you are making a solid effort and committing to wanting to become better.

If you are having serious physical conditions, your doctor might want to put you on medications such as blood pressure medication. While taking medicine though if needed, you can also do some things at home to improve your mind-body connection.

Stress management techniques are one of the top ways you can reduce stress and get your body back into better health. Stress management looks different for everyone, but many people think that practicing a hobby you enjoy can help reduce stress and enlighten your mind.

If you already have a hobby, you can make time to practice it more often. If you don't have a hobby, try and find one. Anything can be a hobby from writing, to reading, to painting. Hobbies can also include physical things such as bike riding, yoga, or running.

One way to improve the mind-body connection is to also practice relaxation techniques. This can include mediation, yoga, or deep breathing. Sitting quietly and breathing deeply can help balance your emotions. If you aren't sure how to do this on your own, there are many videos or books that can help take you through the practice until you get used to doing it on your own.

Investing in you is also the key to being more mindful of the mind-body connection. This means investing in your health in all areas including nutrition, fitness, work, hobbies, and personal relationships. A huge part of investing in you includes finding a good life-work balance.

Without the proper work-life balance, you won't have time for yourself, and this can damage growth and the process of being whole.

The last major part of understanding the mind-body connection is to develop resilience. Part of resilience is to have good social support and to have a positive view of you. If you're able to think positively and be resilient, you will be able to keep things in perspective even when they might not go your way.

The Connection Between Mind and Body

There have been many studies done on the connection between the mind and body. Some scientists and doctors have even done neuroimaging of people's brains during stressful situations or life experiences. During stressful situations, neuroimaging shows that the brain and nervous system actually change.

This means that your behavior actually has the ability to change neuropath ways, whether it is in a good or bad way. This is one of the reasons that many doctors and people believe that medicine is not enough anymore to change certain conditions and illnesses, especially illnesses that are brought on by stress, anxiety, or depression.

Nutrition and the Mind

The things you put into your body matter for your physical and mental health, as well as how they relate to one another. Studies have shown that nutrient-dense food can provide better emotional and mental well being. Since your mind is connected to your body, your mind is also connected to the stomach and the digestive tract.

There is also some evidence that people with diverse and healthy diets also are less likely to suffer from anxiety and depression. The next chapter of the book will go over nutrition and healthy living in greater detail.

Using Yoga and Meditation

Yoga and mediation are one of the top ways to become more in sync with your mind and body connection. Doing yoga activates certain hormones and neurotransmitters that are in charge of relaxing the body and dealing better with stress.

Yoga also does a better job of releasing these neurotransmitters than other exercises like weightlifting or walking. Of course, you can do your regular exercise routines but consider adding in 30 minutes of yoga at the beginning of the end.

Using Positivity

Staying positive and thinking positive is much easier said than done. One way you can make a difference with your thoughts though is to realize that everything is temporary. Thinking more positive doesn't happen every night and it's okay if negative thoughts creep into your mind sometimes. The most important thing to do is just pushing them out and replaces them with better thoughts.

In the moments you are thinking negatively, you can also focus on things you love and enjoy so that your mind can better focus.

Chapter 3. Eat Your Veggies and Get Some Sleep

As a child, you were probably asked to eat your veggies and drink water. They seem like simple practices, but they are easy to fall out of as we grow into adults. Lack of time often makes people eat on the go or too frequently in restaurants. Fast food and food that lacks nutrition are also cheaper; so many people choose to eat these quick foods because they have to or because they are trying to save money.

Being whole physically includes eating healthy though and making better decisions when it comes to food. If you aren't sure what foods to eat for better health, try to buy fresher foods from the produce section of the grocery store rather than boxed or processed foods.

Better food choices include more vegetables, fruits, and lean meats. You can also throw in some nuts, dairy, and whole grains to complete the diet. Another easy way to make sure your diet has variety and nutrients are to make your plate as colorful as possible

For example, when choosing vegetables, you can choose different ones such as green lettuce, yellow bell peppers, avocados, and tomatoes.

Choosing dairy products that are lower in sugar is also a good health choice. You can choose plain yogurt and add in some honey rather than choosing vanilla or strawberry flavored one.

Intuitive Eating

Part of reconnecting with you physically involves intuitive eating. This means eating mindfully and paying attention to hunger cues rather than dieting frequently. Going on diets may work for weight loss or meeting certain nutrition goals, but they often don't give you lifelong health. Part of eating intuitively involves paying attention to your body and rejecting the mentality of needing to diet.

Try to also not label food as good and bad. Everything is okay to eat, especially when you are doing it in moderation. So you don't have to think of cookies or pasta as bad. Instead, view these foods as part of an overall diet. Being free to eat anything gives you more power over your body and food choices.

Keep in mind that intuitive eating is not the best for weight loss. Instead, use intuitive eating as a way to monitor your mental and physical health. People who practice intuitive eating often have better body image, lower levels of depression, and better self-esteem. This is because they feel more in control of their minds and bodies.

Learning to Know Your Internal Signals

You probably already know that your body tells you when you are hungry or full. Because of busy lifestyles, people often ignore these signals and eat only when they have finished working or when the kids are in bed. It's also easy to find yourself gorging on one meal a day because of lack of time or maybe even money.

Try to learn your body signals and respond to them. Even if you are busy at work, try to take a few minutes to eat something small or ask your boss if you can take your lunch break early. You might also need to better manage tasks and goals so that you have more time to eat at work.

Part of knowing your internal signals also involves stopping eating when you are full. The main part of intuitive eating involves knowing when to stop eating. Not only does this keep you from overeating, but it also allows you to be more in tune with your body and the way you are feeling when you are eating.

Starting Intuitive Eating

If you have never tried intuitive eating before, it can be hard to start. You will also need to take some time to discover your eating and food habits. If you find yourself having negative thoughts about food or eating, you might want to consider talking to a nutritionist or dietitian.

You can also join a group for intuitive eating so that you can support one another and share strategies and tips.

Make sure none of the intuitive eating approaches you are taking is dieting. For example, don't start cutting foods or counting calories. Just try to eat foods that matter to you and make sure you are eating when you feel hungry and cutting back when you are feeling full.

The Importance of Sleep

With busy lives and work and school, sometimes getting enough sleep is impossible. While cutting back on sleeping is okay if you need to for a few days, it's not good to lack sleep for long prolonged periods of time, even if it's for school or work.

Part of getting enough sleep means prioritizing sleep and ensuring you are meeting goals and tasks so that you can get enough sleep at night. This also involves a better work-life balance. If you are overworking yourself, you will never be able to get enough sleep.

Sometimes sleep doesn't have to do with how much you are getting, but rather the quality of sleep you are getting. Even if you lay in bed for 8 hours a night, you won't be well rested if you are waking up every hour or if you are having insomnia.

Lack of quality sleep often stems from anxiety or having too much on your brain. This might cause you to wake up frequently or to dream often because you are thinking about things that make you anxious even when you are asleep.

You also need to create a sleep schedule for better sleep. This involves going to bed and waking up every morning at the same time. You can also try meditating or drinking tea before bed. Try to limit screen time before bed as well so that you aren't distracted when trying to fall asleep.

Chapter 4. Don't Be Afraid to Face Your Demons

Past failures and traumas are one of the main reasons why people find it hard to move on from they're past and become whole. These failures and demons must be faced before you can really start to change yourself. Remember that it's perfectly okay to undergo therapy or talk to someone you trust when you need to face your demons. Doing it by you, can be overwhelming and difficult.

You also need to know why you have these inner demons. This means going back in time and realizing what traumas or failures have caused you not to be whole. Inner demons also show up when you are most vulnerable and can cause havoc and chaos in your life. It's important to try and face these demons before you allow them to further attack you.

Understanding Where Inner Demons Come From

Most inner demons come from past failures or rejections. They might also come from self-doubt and negative thinking patterns. Some inner demons can even come from our childhood if we constantly had someone speaking negatively to us.

Inner demons then become stuck in your brain constantly telling you that you are not enough or that you can always be doing better. You need to always be conscious of these thoughts as some people might even be thinking of them and be unaware. These inner negative voices can become so common that we start to just live with them rather than trying to fight back with them.

Responding to the Demons

You might recognize the voices of the demons, but you don't know how to respond to them or take them down. Remember that you have the right to be happy and not to suffer. This means you need to face the demons with positivity.

Doing this looks different for everyone. First, though, you need to face the demons head-on. Identify your trauma and then get ready to tell the demons off. This is different than just ignoring the demons or stuffing the voices into the back of your head. This might work for a little while, but it never ends well.

You need to use the truth to quieten the demons. Respond to them with positivity and affirming words such as telling them that you are good enough or do you have a reason to be proud of all your accomplishments. These inner demons will try and tell you otherwise. Don't let them.

Don't Ignore the Demons

It's important not to ignore the demons as this is not effectively responding to them and overcoming them. The demons and critical voices in your head sometimes have something important to tell you. They might also tell you something about yourself that you need to listen to you. This allows you to tap into your past trauma and learn how it has affected you and made you not whole.

Listening to the inner demons can also help you realize your fears, even the ones you have pushed back into your subconscious. Make sure not to listen to them for too long though. Once you have heard what they have to say though, you can fight them much easier and win.

Concentrate on the Good

Remembering all the good things in your life can help you to face your inner demons as well. When you hear those voices swarming around you, try and get back into a happy place by focusing on good times and good memories.

Some people also find it helpful to make lists of things that make them happy. You can also make a list of things you feel grateful for. This will help you to concentrate on the good and be able to get past the inner demons that might be always stuck in your head trying to bring you down.

Always Cut Yourself Some Slack

Oftentimes, we can be too hard on ourselves. When we start to tune in too much to these inner demons, it can be easy to only remember our downfalls or the areas where we think we fail. Always remember that you're human and you will make mistakes, big ones, and small ones.

Let Positive Emotions Take Control

While it's normal to feel down and negative during the times your inner demons want to take control, you can also try to push those emotions away with positivity and light. Allow you to breathe into the negativity and then allow yourself to start to push it away with good thoughts and emotions.

We stated earlier that you shouldn't ignore the demons, but you do need to make sure you are not letting them take control and determine your thoughts and actions.

Taming or Killing the Demons

When you are ready to get rid of those inner demons and not let them rule your life anymore, you have two choices. You can either tame them or kill them. If these demons have been around your whole life, killing them might prove to be more difficult because you can have a hard time letting them go.

Taming the inner demons can be easier. Taming them means overpowering their voices with your one true voice. This is all part of getting rid of the negative thoughts with more positive ones.

Counseling and Therapy

During the process of getting rid of inner demons, many people find it helpful to seek therapy or counseling. This can be costly though. If you are wanting to seek counseling but lack the funds, try checking local churches or social work offices, as these places often give a few sessions for free. If you are in college, many university centers also give free counseling to students.

Counseling is best for those who want to seek professional guidance and for those who do not want to include family and friends. If you want to talk to a relative or friend though, that's perfectly okay. It all depends on what you are comfortable with.

Chapter 5. Lean on Faith

Part of becoming whole also means focusing on your spirituality. This looks different for everyone depending on what faith or religion you are a part of. You might not be part of faith, but are looking to get involved with one as part of your spiritual journey.

No matter where your faith might lie, leaning on faith is an important part of becoming whole spiritually.

People, who attend church services, find it helpful to read their Bibles often during difficult times because God can speak to them through the passages and stories found in the Bible. If you are Christian, you might find that having weekly devotions helps you. This involves reading your Bible and spending some quiet time with God.

Some people also choose to do their weekly devotions in a group. This can be done through the church or you can find some people and create your group at your home. To lean on your faith and create a closer relationship with God, you can also do weekly group devotions and solo daily devotions.

If you aren't sure how to read the Bible or how to start, there are many different devotion books you can purchase that can take you through the Bible. You can also buy specialty devotion books aimed at helping you lean on faith and getting to know God better.

If you are not part of a church or devotion group, becoming part of one is the first step to making sure you are growing and becoming whole spiritually. You can research churches in your area and attend a service to get more involved. Some churches even have small groups where you can get better connected to people in the church that are the same age or in the same walk of life as you.

Using Music

No matter what religion or faith you might follow, using music is a healthy way to learn more about faith. You can use Spotify or another music streaming service to make playlists or download music that you feel aligns with your faith. Make sure to have the playlist handy whenever you might be feeling down or when you think you need help leaning on your faith.

You can also play the music before stressful situations, such as when you are headed to work or when you are anxious about an event or meeting that is coming up. Filling your heart with spiritual music helps you become more in tune with your faith.

Talking to Other Believers

If you are part of organized religion, you might have a group of fellow believers that you know can help you lean on your faith better. If you have someone that you trust in this group, you can ask to meet with them and you can share why you might be struggling to lean on your faith. You can also share with them that you are on a journey to become more whole spiritually.

Other believers will be able to offer tips and advice to help you. They might also have books or things they have used in the past that can help you lean on your faith.

Setting Aside Your Emotions

In many cases, when you are struggling with faith, it's because you have unsettled emotions. For example, you might be angry with God for something or you might not understand why your spiritual practices are not helping you.

These negative emotions can get in the way of you leaning and relying on faith. Sometimes emotions can also mislead you because you might expect a certain outcome from your faith, but things do not always turn out the way you expect them to.

Instead of expecting things from faith and letting your emotions get in the way, try to just let faith lead you. Focus more on the experience and the growth rather than the final outcome.

Participate in Services

Depending on your spiritual practice, there might be services or groups you can get involved with. Fellowship is an important part of most faiths and religions. Being around other people that believe the same things as you can help you get some perspective on your trials and how to use faith to overcome them.

Pray

If prayer is part of your spiritual walk, praying can be a good way to lean more into your faith. Many people find it helpful to pray at the same time every day such as first thing when you wake up or before you go to bed. You can also use prayer time to reflect and listen.

Some people also use prayer journals as a way to keep track of their prayers and when they are answered. Prayer journals are also nice to go back and reflect on when you need to so that you can see what trials you were facing and how you got through them.

Even though it's a good idea to make a habit of praying at the same time every day, you can pray whenever you want or feel like you need to. Praying is a great way to connect and to let out your worries and frustrations.

Listen to Podcasts

There are many different podcasts aimed at religion and spirituality. You can listen to a few a week to grow yourself spiritually. Podcasts are great to listen to when driving or when cleaning or picking up around the house. They can give you guidance when you need it. Make sure you are reading the reviews of the podcasts to choose a good one that you can trust.

Chapter 6 Habits are the Building Blocks of Life

If you want to become whole and create a new lifestyle, it's important to have good habits that push you towards your goals. Bad habits can be detrimental, so you also need to break them if you have them.

Habits are formed by experiences that we have even started in very early life. We often repeat these experiences or things until they become habits. Once a habit has started to be performed automatically, it can be very hard to break or change. That's why it's important to try and form good habits only.

You might have certain life habits that you aren't even aware of, such as brushing your teeth every morning or turning on the coffee machine. You might also have bad habits that you don't realize, such as watching TV while working or making excuses for not exercising or making it to the gym.

Habits as the Keys to Health

Habits are a big part of every aspect of health including mentally, physically, and spiritually. For example, praying daily might be a spiritual habit you have. Exercising every day is a physical habit you might have developed throughout the years.

There are many habits you can create, such as eating better and not consuming soda that is important to overall health.

Healthy habits can affect you physically by allowing you to keep a healthy weight, keep your blood sugar in check, and lower your risk of chronic diseases.

Mental habits and spiritual habits are just as important as physical ones. Spiritual habits night include prayer, devotions, religious services, or listening to music. Mental habits can involve anything that helps your mental health such as doing a hobby, practicing yoga, or just having quiet time with yourself to reflect.

The Power of Habits and Routines

Every day from the time you wake up until the time you go to bed, you are constantly making decisions. Some decisions are small and might not seem to make a difference in your daily routine, but every choice you make has the ability to affect your day and life altogether.

Routines can help ground you and will help you to have special habits within those routines. For example, if you have an alarm every morning for 7 am, your body will naturally fall into that routine and wake up to the sound of the alarm. This is a habit and a routine you have created for yourself.

Having routines and habits also takes away some of the weight of making daily decisions that you might experience. If you make it a habit to make coffee at home every morning, this takes away the decision of stopping by the local coffee shop and spending more money.

Making Routines Centered Around a Goal

If you don't have a lot of routines or habits already, you might be thinking about how to make them. One easy way to make routines is to think of goals you might have and then make routines to reach those goals. If you have a goal to save money for the next months, make it part of your routine to prep lunch for work the day before instead of going out for lunch every day.

If you have a goal to run a half marathon, you need to make it part of your routine to run most days of the week. If you don't have a goal, you need to make some before making habits and routines. Having goals is very important when it comes to accomplishing things throughout life.

How to Choose Goals and Tasks

If you are having a hard time prioritizing goals and making concrete plans, you can try to do the most important tasks rather than the most urgent ones. Not everything in life that is urgent is important. Choosing which tasks to complete is part of a time management system you need to have in your work and home life.

For example, your boss might have a task for you that are urgent, but it requires you to stay at work late and miss dinners with your kids and spouse. While having a family dinner is not urgent, it is valued as more important as a work task.

This is part of the bigger habit of creating work-life balance though which is hard for some people. Depending on your job, you might be required to work late or miss things with the family. Consider ways you can change this. It might involve talking to your boss and working out a different work schedule. Don't be afraid to make a work-life balance. Draining yourself at work can be detrimental to every other aspect of your life.

Establishing Habits and Routines

An easy way to make routines is to put time around them. For example, make a morning routine if you don't already have one. This might include simple tasks like brushing your teeth, making coffee, getting the kids dressed, and making a simple breakfast for everyone.

If you need to make different routines and habits for your days, you can start by making small adjustments to the routines you already have. For example, maybe you get up early and have a morning routine, but you don't eat breakfast and you want to start.

You can make adjustments such as getting up earlier or prepping your breakfast the night before so you have time to eat in the morning. Making small adjustments to the routines you already have can be easier than creating new routines completely.

Once you're comfortable with small adjustments, you can start to add more. You can also completely change the routine once you feel comfortable doing so.

Analyzing Habits and Routines

With existing and new routines, they need to be analyzed and recreated if there are issues. Reflecting on your routines is important because you want to make sure they are actually adding value and purpose to your life.

Ask yourself what purpose the routines serve in your life and what difference they make to your overall health. Ask yourself if the goal is working. If it's not, you need to think of ways that you can make it work. If you can't make it work, you need to change that part of the routine into something that does work.

Remember that routines should have goals. You shouldn't have routines just to have routines. Goals can be simple though. For example, you have a habit of brushing your teeth every morning because you have a goal of keeping good oral health and spending less money at the dentist.

Not every goal has to be complex. You do need to think about the goal of each routine you have though to make sure the routine is serving a purpose.

Chapter 7 Don't Isolate Yourself

Becoming whole might seem like a personal journey, and in many ways it is. That doesn't mean you need to do it all by yourself though. Doing anything, by you, can be difficult and maybe even impossible in some cases.

To really focus on yourself, you also need to focus on others. You also need to ensure there are other people focused on you and your journey to being whole.

Being isolated and lonely can even have mental and physical consequences. Research has shown that isolating and being alone for long periods of time increases your chances of obesity, heart disease, depression, and anxiety. To achieve true health and wellbeing, you need to have people on your team and you need to have people invested in you.

The Importance of Having People in Your Life

When people think of wanting to have a support team, they often think of friends and family. Everyone on your support team needs to be someone you trust and respect. While it might seem like you need to involve the family in everything, this isn't true if you have relatives that do not uplift you and build you up. The same rule goes for friends. You only need to invite friends that are truly there for you and have your best interest in mind.

Some people also turn to their religious or spiritual groups to find support and to avoid isolation. If you are on a sports team or have coworkers that you have trust, you can also include them in your support system.

The Importance of Fellowship

Being around other people is important for all parts of health. Having friends and people you trust can make you feel less alone and give you room to grow with other people. Fellowship can also give you people in your life that can give you advice and tips. All these things are important for being whole and for being in optimal health.

Isolation can make you feel like you have no one to turn to in times of need, which can cause you to make rash and poor decisions. When you are making big life choices, it's always good to discuss them with people in your life. If you are isolated, getting help when you need it might be impossible.

Creating Boundaries

Even though you need to have a support team and people on your side, you do not have to include them in everything. You can make boundaries on what you want people to know and what you prefer to keep to yourself. Make sure the people in your support group know these boundaries and that they should never cross them.

You might also have boundaries for some people that don't exist for others. For example, you might have some people in your life that do not support your religion or spiritual life because theirs might be different. In this case, you might not share your spiritual journey with them, but rather than just the mental and physical aspects of your journey to be whole.

Sometimes It's Okay to Be Alone

You don't always have to be around people though. Sometimes you need space to be alone with your thoughts and emotions. Even though you have talked through your problems with people before, you might want to still take time to think about them alone too.

The easiest way to think about is that solitude is okay, but isolation is not. Solitude just means you have chosen to spend time alone. Isolation means you have cut people out of your life or pushed people away.

Solitude is okay when it's voluntary and when you still have positive relationships in your life that you can turn to when times get difficult. You will also have social groups to interact with when you choose. You also need to feel good about spending time alone.

Choosing to be alone and learning to be alone can be rejuvenating and refreshing. Make sure you are doing something you love during your alone time so that your mind and body begin to feel better about being alone.

Rejoin Social Groups Often

Some people can become too comfortable being alone. Being alone is great sometimes, but it's not ideal to be alone all the time, especially for your journey to becoming whole. If you find yourself spending too much time alone, make sure to rejoin your social groups or create an event to get some friends together.

You can also create social groups around your health. For example, you can make a gym or running group make it easy to get physically fit. You can also make a spiritual group such as a weekly devotional group at your home.

Chapter 8 Mastering Your Health is a Journey

Just when you have everything in your journey or life figured out, something comes along and changes everything. This is why your health is a journey and not a destination. You will always have more work to do because life changes quickly.

All parts of your health are a journey, whether it is spiritual, mental, or physical. Everyone's journey is also unique, so yours will not look the same as other people. Try not to compare other journeys to yours.

Health is also evolving, so you will need to make changes to your life and routines as life changes. You can master your health, but you need to be willing to work and put in the effort every day. Good health is also a process from the very start.

Enjoying the Journey

The journey might be hard sometimes, but you need to make sure you are making space to enjoy it and appreciate it. Even if you have mastered your health, you might still find yourself making choices that are not ideal such as making poor food choices or skipping exercise routines for a few days or weeks.

Once you have fallen out of a routine, it can be very hard to get back into it. That's why you always need to push yourself and make sure you are not falling out of routines. If you are, you need to make sure you get back onto your feet as soon as possible.

No matter what, enjoy the journey though. Even if you have aimed to eat healthily, you also need to have days where you enjoy meals including dessert and snacks. This is part of enjoying life. You also need to learn to enjoy the ups and downs of life.

If you are only concentrating on the ups of life and let yourself get down when life throws things your way, you can find yourself stuck in a rut. Even when less than ideal things come into life, try to take a deep breath and enjoy each day as it comes.

Understanding Your Journey

Your journey will look different than everyone else's. This is because we are all unique and special in our own ways. That means you need to always look inward when understanding your journey and the way it happens.

When you fall along with hardship or something else that might put a roadblock in your journey, you need to stop and think about why these things are happening and what you can do to overcome them sooner. Each part of your journey is a process.

Remember that you also need to learn new things during your journey. Each hardship will teach you something you need to know about your life or as a person. Hardships might also teach you something you need to know about other people to help them in their experiences or issues.

Everything is Connected

Just as the body is connected and all works together, your journey to health is also connected. One thing can affect other parts, whether it is good or bad. Understanding that everything is connected can help you to become whole and heal. As your mental health becomes whole, your physical and spiritual health will also be one step closer to being whole as well.

Setting goals will also show you that everything is connected because it will show you how accomplishing one goal leads you closer and closer to the next goal.

Don't Think About Failure

Since you have learned that health is a journey and there will be hardships, you might be thinking that failure is inevitable. This is not true though and failure is not synonymous with hardships. You will encounter many different hardships and trials, but this does mean you will fail.

When hardship comes along, don't immediately think that failure is the next step. Just take each step and day as it comes and enjoy the ride. Remember that failure will only happen if you allow it. And if you happen to fail at one part of the journey, this does not mean you will fail at the entire journey. As long as you get up and keep moving, you can be sure you will succeed.

Keep Self Care Practices and Routines

As part of your health journey, you will need to make sure you are keeping your routines and self-care. If you don't keep the practices during your hardships and trials, you will find that succeeding is much harder.

Self-care also involves reflecting and doing something you love during hardships. This can be anything from reading to swimming to doing a facial or a massage. This will help you to work through the problem at hand and realize concrete solutions that can get you past the hump and on the other side.

This is also part of why having people in your corner is super important in overcoming hardships. If you are feeling like you might be close to failure, you need to make sure you are reaching out to your support group and asking them for help. Share your feelings and fears and see how they can advise you.

Chapter 9 Conclusion

Being whole doesn't happen overnight and it takes practice and effort. If you are wanting to become whole though, it's probably because you have experienced something in life that has affected you negatively whether it be spiritually, physically, or mentally. If this is the case, we hope this book has taught you ways to work towards becoming more whole and overcoming hardships that might have been affecting you.

Remember that every journey starts with one small step. You need to take a small step to get towards the bigger steps that are needed to have a journey of faith and self-fulfillment. Once you have made one small step, these steps will eventually turn into habits and routines, which can change your life forever.

Part of being whole also involves the mind-body connection. Every thought you have affects your body in some way, whether it is negative or positive. Negative thoughts can even make you feel ill or run down.

Eating healthy and getting quality sleep is also part of being whole. With the right nutrition and sleep, you can be more aware of how you feel mentally and physically.

The last parts of being whole involve finding a support group and leaning on your faith during the hard times. Remember that being whole also means you are on a constant journey.

www.ingramcontent.com/pod-product-compliance
Lightning Source LLC
LaVergne TN
LVHW021312160826
845679LV00001B/322

* 9 7 9 8 8 2 0 9 3 1 9 7 0 *